Let's Go Invent Tomorrow

Other Books in the In Their Own Words Series

Rocket Man: Elon Musk In His Own Words
Own It: Oprah Winfrey In Her Own Words
Never Give Up: Jack Ma In His Own Words
The Google Boys: Sergey Brin and Larry Page In Their Own Words
The World's Richest Man: Carlos Slim In His Own Words
Virgin Rebel: Richard Branson In His Own Words
The Boy Billionaire: Mark Zuckerberg In His Own Words
The Oracle Speaks: Warren Buffett In His Own Words
Impatient Optimist: Bill Gates In His Own Words
I, Steve: Steve Jobs In His Own Words

Let's Go Invent Tomorrow

A Year's Worth of Quotes, Wisdom, and Insight
from the World's Most Successful Business Leaders

Edited by Jessica Easto

AN AGATE IMPRINT

CHICAGO

Printed in the United States

Portions of this book have appeared in previously published volumes in the In Their Own Words series.

Let's Go Invent Tomorrow
ISBN 13: 978-1-57284-232-8
ISBN 10: 1-57284-232-6
eISBN 13: 978-1-57284-810-8
eISBN 10: 1-57284-810-3
First printing: September 2017

10 9 8 7 6 5 4 3 2 1   17 18 19 20 21

B2 Books is an imprint of Agate Publishing. Agate books are available in bulk at discount prices. For more information, visit agatepublishing.com.

To those
who dare
and act

PREFACE

In 2011, Agate started publishing books of quotations from the world's most successful entrepreneurs and business leaders, trusting that their advice and insights might prove valuable to readers who owned businesses, managed teams, or were aspiring to launch a new venture. Our first volume, *I, Steve: Steve Jobs In His Own Words*, went on to become a *New York Times* bestseller, and we have since put out nine more books, each highlighting the captivating, inspiring words of one of the most fascinating business icons of the last 50 years.

Let's Go Invent Tomorrow is a carefully curated collection of the most illuminating quotes from the In Their Own Words series. In these pages, you'll find a full year's worth of expert advice on leadership, management, business, success, failure, and much more. This handy little book is a daily dose of inspiration from a virtual chorus of visionaries—Warren Buffett, Bill Gates, Jack Ma, and Oprah Winfrey, among others.

These entrepreneurs come from diverse backgrounds and bring a sundry of personal and business interests to the table—we were struck both by the opinions many of them share as well as those they don't. As we edited the book, we realized that *Let's Go Invent Tomorrow* puts these great business thinkers into conversation with each other, adding a thought-provoking layer to our series.

Whether you have just finished school and are on the verge of starting a career, in the midst of your professional life, or harboring a desire to start your own business, we hope this book will help you think about your own goals and dreams in a new light. After all, anything can happen in a year. What will you achieve?

—Jessica Easto, Editor

BIOGRAPHIES

Richard Branson (BORN JULY 18, 1950) is an investor and the founder of Virgin Group, a venture capital conglomerate. Virgin Group began with the Virgin Records music stores and label in 1972 and has since expanded into the Virgin Atlantic airline, the Virgin Galactic space tourism company, and Virgin Mobile cellular service, among others.

Sergey Brin (BORN AUGUST 21, 1973) created Google, the most popular search engine in the world, with Larry Page in 1998. Brin is currently the president of Alphabet, Google's parent company.

Warren Buffett (BORN AUGUST 30, 1930) is an investor and the chairman of Berkshire Hathaway, a conglomerate holding company with full or partial ownership of Coca-Cola, Geico, Wells Fargo, Apple Computer, and many other major corporations.

Bill Gates (BORN OCTOBER 28, 1955) started Microsoft, now the world's largest PC software company, in 1975 with Paul Allen. Although Gates still serves on the board of Microsoft, much of his time is now spent on the Bill and Melinda Gates Foundation, a philanthropic organization he founded with his wife Melinda Gates in 2000.

Steve Jobs (FEBRUARY 24, 1955–OCTOBER 5, 2011) founded Apple Computer with Steve Wozniak in 1976. Although he left the company in 1985, Jobs returned in 1997 to help pilot Apple back to popularity, introducing such products and services as the iPhone, iPod, Macbook Pro, and iTunes. Jobs passed away in 2011 after a decade-long battle with pancreatic cancer.

Jack Ma (BORN SEPTEMBER 10, 1964) is the cofounder and executive chairman of Alibaba Group, a Chinese conglomerate of internet-based businesses. Alibaba, an e-commerce platform and the world's largest retailer, is the cornerstone of the Alibaba Group.

Elon Musk (BORN JUNE 28, 1971) is the CEO of Tesla Motors, which manufactures and sells electric cars, and the CEO and founder of SpaceX, which aims to build reusable rockets intended for space exploration. Musk's other ventures and ideas include Hyperloop, a high-speed transportation system; SolarCity, a solar energy company; and Neuralink, a proposed fusion of the human brain with artificial intelligence.

Larry Page (BORN MARCH 26, 1973) created Google, the most popular search engine in the world, with Sergey Brin in 1998. Page now serves as the CEO of Alphabet, Google's parent company.

Carlos Slim (BORN JANUARY 28, 1940) is an investor and the founder of conglomerate holding group Grupo Carso. Grupo Carso has holdings in the telecommunications, media, real estate, technology, and transportation sectors, among others.

Oprah Winfrey (BORN JANUARY 29, 1954) first rose to fame in the 1980s with *The Oprah Winfrey Show*, the highest-rated talk show in American history. Since the finale of that show in 2011, Winfrey has turned the focus on the rest of her media empire, which includes the Oprah Winfrey Network, *O, The Oprah Magazine*, Oprah Radio, and appearances in film, television, and books.

Mark Zuckerberg (BORN MAY 14, 1984) cofounded Facebook as a Harvard college student in 2004. Facebook is now one of the most popular social networks in the world, with over 1.86 billion active monthly users. Zuckerberg currently serves as the chairman and CEO of Facebook.

1

THE **FIRST STEP** IS TO ESTABLISH THAT SOMETHING IS POSSIBLE; THEN PROBABILITY WILL OCCUR.

ELON MUSK
Esquire, 2012

2

I think it is often easier to make progress on mega-ambitious dreams. I know that sounds completely nuts. But since no one else is crazy enough to do it, you have little competition. There are so few people this crazy that I feel like I know them all by first name. They all travel as if they are pack dogs and stick to each other like glue. **The best people want to work the big challenges.**

LARRY PAGE
commencement address at the University of Michigan, 2009

3

It's rare for me or the team to consider only the money that can be made. I feel it's pointless to approach investing with the question, "How can I make lots of money?"

RICHARD BRANSON
Like a Virgin, 2012

4

Entrepreneurs
should be guided
by responsibility
and teamwork,
not money. True
entrepreneurs don't
think of money first
but only about their
dream to start a
company. **Money is
the final element.**

JACK MA
APEC's 5th e-Business Champions Grand Awards Ceremony, 2008

5

I was worth about over a million dollars when I was twenty-three and over ten million dollars when I was twenty-four, and over a hundred million dollars when I was twenty-five, and it wasn't that important because *I never did it for the money*.

STEVE JOBS
Triumph of the Nerds, 1996

6

Even today, what interests me isn't making money per se. If I had to choose between my job and having great wealth, **I'D CHOOSE THE JOB**. It's a much bigger thrill to lead a team of thousands of talented, bright people than it is to have a big bank account.

BILL GATES
New York Times, 1996

7

You always hear the phrase "Money doesn't buy you happiness." But I always, in the back of my mind, figured a lot of money will buy you a little bit of happiness. **But it's not really true.** I got a new car because the old one's lease expired. Nothing terribly fancy—you could drive the same car.

SERGEY BRIN
Time, 2006

8

Money's only interesting for what it lets you do. On paper, if I was to sell up my shareholdings in the companies tomorrow, I would have considerable wealth. **But where would be the fun in that?**

RICHARD BRANSON
Business Stripped Bare, 2008

9

What money does is magnify you.
Whatever kind of person you are
going in—and age does this too
as people get older—it magnifies
both . . . good and bad tendencies.
Money gives you a chance if you're
a slob to be a big slob—a huge slob.
On the other hand, if you're inclined
toward doing good things, it gives
you the power to do a great many
great things.

WARREN BUFFETT
Georgia Tech Alumni Magazine, 2003

10

When you get to my age, you'll really measure success in life by how many of the people you want to have love you actually do love you. I know people who have a lot of money, and they get testimonial dinners and they get hospital wings named after them. But the truth is that nobody in the world loves them. If you get to my age in life and nobody thinks well of you, I don't care how big your bank account is, [your life] is a disaster.

WARREN BUFFETT
Georgia Tech Alumni Magazine, 2003

11

*It's not about the money,
it's about the dreams.
It's not only about the
technology that will
change the world.*
**It's about the dreams
you believe that
change the world.**

JACK MA
Economic Club of New York, 2015

12

Sure, what we do has
to make commercial
sense, but it's never
the starting point.
**We start with the
product and the user
experience.**

Time, 2010

13

It's better to approach
this [building a company]
from the standpoint
of saying—rather than
you want to be an
entrepreneur or you want
to make money—what
are some useful things
that you do that you wish
existed in the world?

ELON MUSK
Boao Forum for Asia, 2015

14

BUSINESS IS WHAT
CONCERNS US. IF
YOU CARE ABOUT
SOMETHING ENOUGH
TO DO SOMETHING
ABOUT IT, YOU'RE IN
BUSINESS.

RICHARD BRANSON
Richard's blog, 2012

15

You must be ready to bear the pressure, criticism, and loneliness that come with being an innovator. **At first we were called cheaters, then crazy, and now complete lunatics.** No matter what other people say, however, we believe in our company and ourselves. I don't care how others look at us but rather how we look at the world.

JACK MA
CCTV Innovation Forum, 2005

16

[Success is] also a timeliness thing; everyone said Sam Walton was crazy to build big stores in small towns. Almost everyone who has had an idea that's somewhat revolutionary or wildly successful was first told they're **insane**.

LARRY PAGE
Fortune, 2008

17

People are
going to
second-guess
anything you
do.

BILL GATES
Newsweek, 1999

18

As you get older, your obligations increase. And once you have a family, you start taking risks not just for yourself but for your family as well. It gets much harder to do things that might not work out. So now is the time to do that—before you have those obligations. I would encourage you to take risks now; **do something bold**. You won't regret it.

ELON MUSK
commencement address at the University of Southern California, 2014

19

A little blindness is necessary when you undertake a risk. *You have to have a little suspension of disbelief where you say, "Hey, we're going to do this unproven product. Let's do our best."*

BILL GATES
Costco Connection, 1997

20

The biggest risk is not taking
any risk. . . . In the world that
changes really quickly, the only
strategy that is guaranteed to
fail is not taking risks.

MARK ZUCKERBERG
Startup School, 2011

21

Only the ones
that don't make
decisions, don't
make mistakes. But
the worst mistake
is to not make a
decision.

CARLOS SLIM
WTTC Americas Summit, 2012

22

So many businesses get worried about looking like they might make a mistake, they become afraid to take any risk. **Companies are set up so that people judge each other on failure.** I'm not going to get fired if we have a bad year. Or a bad five years. I don't have to worry about making things look good if they're not. I can actually set up the company to create value.

MARK ZUCKERBERG
Fast Company, 2012

23

You need to do stuff you are passionate about. The companies that work are the ones that people really care about and have a vision for the world, so **do something you like**.

Startup School, 2011

24

I'm convinced that about half of what separates the successful entrepreneurs from the non-successful ones is *pure perseverance*. . . . Unless you have a lot of passion about this, you're not going to survive. You're going to give it up. So you've got to have an idea, or a problem or a wrong that you want to right that you're passionate about; otherwise, you're not going to have the perseverance to stick it through.

STEVE JOBS
Smithsonian Institution Oral and Video Histories, 1995

25

You can have vision
but unless you
maintain leadership
of the vision and are
there to help oversee
the execution of the
vision, it doesn't work.

OPRAH WINFREY
The Hollywood Reporter, 2012

26

THERE IS A VERY THIN DIVIDING LINE BETWEEN SUCCESS AND FAILURE.

RICHARD BRANSON
Big Think, 2011

27

If something's
important
enough, you
should try. Even
if the probable
outcome is failure.

ELON MUSK
60 Minutes, 2014

28

Nearly a decade
of entrepreneurial
experience tells me these
difficult times can't be
evaded or shouldered by
others—the entrepreneur
must be able to face
failure and never give up.

JACK MA
interview on CCTV website, 2004

29

There's a lot of sad stories about inventors like Nikola Tesla, amazing people who didn't have much impact, because they never turned their inventions into businesses.

LARRY PAGE
Wired, 2013

30

The key is not to worry about being successful but to instead *work toward being significant*—and the success will naturally follow. How can you serve your way to greatness?

OPRAH WINFREY
O, The Oprah Magazine, 2001

31

For me, it was always unsatisfying if you look at companies that get very big and they're just doing one thing. Ideally, if you have more people and more resources, you can get more things solved. We've kind of always had that philosophy.

LARRY PAGE
Time, 2013

32

Wall Street makes its money on activity. You make your money on inactivity. If everybody in this room trades their portfolio around every day with every other person, you're all going to end up broke. The intermediary is going to end up with all the money. On the other hand, if you all own stock in a group of average businesses and just sit here for the next 50 years, you'll end up with a fair amount of money and your broker will be broke.

WARREN BUFFETT
colloquium at the University of Florida, 1998

33

Confirm what should be done to realize your dream. Often this involves taking a step back and letting something go. And be ready to give back and share with others at crucial moments.

JACK MA
Shenzhen Network Operators Meeting, 2008

34

We're all
confused
about
fame
versus
service
in this
country.

OPRAH WINFREY
The Oprah Winfrey Show, 2011

35

Whenever we
make a change,
we try to apply
the lessons we've
learned along
the way.

MARK ZUCKERBERG
Washington Post, 2010

36

For a lot of companies, it's useful for them to feel like they have an obvious competitor and to rally around that. I personally believe that it's better to shoot higher. You don't want to be looking at your competitors. **You want to be looking at what's possible and how to make the world better.**

LARRY PAGE
Bloomberg Businessweek, 2012

37

We try to understand what other people are doing, even if their apparent mission is so distant that it is not obvious competition.

BILL GATES
New York Times, 1996

38

If our competitor is loaded with bullets, we'll try to get him to shoot them into a wall. With the right strategy, **competition should be an amusement, a game—not a source of pain**. Conceiving the strategy of this game unites your employees and you. Remember, the first to lose their temper, loses the game.

JACK MA
Shanghai Network Operators Meeting, 2005

39

COMPETITION MAKES YOU BETTER, ALWAYS, ALWAYS MAKES YOU BETTER, **EVEN IF THE COMPETITOR WINS**.

CARLOS SLIM

Carlosslim.com, 2007

40

If all your competitors are banding together to sort of attack you, that's a good compliment, I think. A very sincere compliment.

ELON MUSK
Countdown to the Closing Bell, 2014

41

Reed College at that time
offered perhaps the best
calligraphy instruction in the
country. . . . I decided to take a
calligraphy class to learn how
to do this. . . . It was beautiful,
historical, artistically subtle in a
way that science can't capture,
and I found it fascinating.
None of this had even a hope
of any practical application
in my life. But ten years later,
when we were designing the
first Macintosh computer, it all
came back to me.

STEVE JOBS
commencement address at Stanford University, 2005

42

The lessons I learned from the dark days at Alibaba are that you've got to make your team have value, innovation, and vision. Also, if you don't give up, you still have a chance. And, when you are small, you have to be very focused and rely on your brain, not your strength.

JACK MA
Inc., 2008

43

Our goal is never to build something cool; it's to build something **useful**. Something that's cool is not going to be around for a long time. Something that's useful is around for a very long time potentially, if it continues to be useful.

MARK ZUCKERBERG
Computer History Museum, 2010

44

When you need others
to say good things
about you, you will have
a problem, because that
has no end. If you need
others to say, "Oh, that's
great!" there is no limit.

CARLOS SLIM
Academy of Achievement, 2007

45

The important thing is to know what you know and know what you don't know. If you can extend the field of things that you know then so much the better.... **There is no use letting your ego tell you that you are good at something that you are not.** To the extent that I can draw that line accurately I'll do well, and to the extent that I won't, I won't.

WARREN BUFFETT
Haaretz, 2011

46

The important
comments come
from your clients—
if users find your
service useful,
then it is. If they
say it's useless, no
matter what you
say about it, it is.

JACK MA
Xiamen Network Operators Meeting, 2001

47

My philosophy is that everything
starts with a great product. So,
you know, I obviously believed
in listening to customers, but
customers can't tell you about the
next breakthrough that's going
to happen next year that's going
to change the whole industry....
But then you have to go and sort
of stow away—you have to go
hide away with people that really
understand the technology, but also
really care about the customers, and
dream up this next breakthrough.

STEVE JOBS
Newsweek, 1985

48

IT IS UNUSUAL TO
HAVE SO MUCH
LUCK IN ONE LIFE, I
THINK. BUT IT'S BEEN
A MAJOR FACTOR IN
WHAT I HAVE BEEN
ABLE TO DO.

BILL GATES
CNBC town hall meeting, 2009

49

I don't believe in luck. For me, **luck is preparation meeting the moment of opportunity.** *There is no luck without you being prepared to handle that moment of opportunity.*

OPRAH WINFREY
Oprah's Master Class, 2011

50

We have a very flat organization. Sometimes ideas flow down, sometimes they flow up, or horizontally. Usually, someone will get an idea or identify a problem and send e-mail to someone else. This may kick off a SWAT team to deal with it. At some point, the decision gets made face to face or over e-mail. On strategic decisions, it may go to a senior VP or to me. **By and large, we empower people to make decisions themselves.**

BILL GATES
Information Outlook, 1997

51

We both respect each other's opinions a lot, so either one of us will make decisions. Usually you have decision paralysis, but we tend to be consistent enough and trust each other enough that we're able to do that. That allows for much better decisions, because you have two heads instead of one. The CEO is such an important, high-level position. Why not have two people do it? Most peoples' ego gets in the way.

LARRY PAGE
interview for FT Dynamo, 2001

52

We tell people that
if no one laughs
at at least one of
their ideas, they're
probably not being
creative enough.

BILL GATES
New York Times, 1996

53

A lot of people think that innovation is just having your great idea. But a lot of it is just moving quickly and trying a lot of things.

MARK ZUCKERBERG
Fast Company: 30 Second MBA, 2012

54

Establish an **expectation of innovation**, and the compensation structure must reflect that. There must also be an allowance for failure because if you are trying something new, necessarily there is some chance it will not work.

ELON MUSK
Offshore Northern Seas, 2014

55

My experience is that when people are trying to do ambitious things, they're all worried about failing when they start. But all sorts of interesting things spin out that are of huge economic value. Also, in these kinds of projects, you get to work with the best people and have a very interesting time. They're not really taking a risk, but they feel like they are.

LARRY PAGE
Fortune, 2008

56

Victory in our industry is spelled *survival*. The way we're going to survive is to innovate our way out of this.

STEVE JOBS
Time, 2002

57

I do think it's worth thinking about whether what you're doing is going to result in disruptive change or not. If it's just incremental, it's unlikely to be something major. It's got to be something that's **substantially better** than what's gone on before.

ELON MUSK
SXSW Conference, 2013

58

Many years ago, I wanted
to change the world.
Now I think if we want
to change the world we
must **change ourselves**.
Changing ourselves is
more important and easier
than changing the world.

JACK MA
World Economic Forum, 2015

59

WHAT IS THE ONE-SENTENCE SUMMARY OF HOW YOU CHANGE THE WORLD? **ALWAYS WORK HARD ON SOMETHING UNCOMFORTABLY EXCITING!**

LARRY PAGE
commencement address at the University of Michigan, 2009

60

I don't think
everything needs to
change the world,
you know. . . . Just say:
"Is what I'm doing as
useful as it could be?"

ELON MUSK
STVP Future Fest, 2015

61

[Technology] doesn't change the world. It really doesn't. Technologies can make it easier, can let us touch people we might not otherwise. But it's a disservice to constantly put things in a radical new light, that it's going to change everything. *Things don't have to change the world to be important.*

STEVE JOBS
Wired, 1996

62

Companies tend to get comfortable doing what they've always done, with a few minor tweaks. It's only natural to want to work on the things you know. But incremental improvement is guaranteed to be obsolete over time.

LARRY PAGE
Google Q1 earnings call, 2013

63

We're gambling
on our vision, and
we would rather
do that than make
"me, too" products.
Let some other
companies do that.
**For us, it's
always the next
dream.**

STEVE JOBS
Apple product event for the first Macintosh computer, 1984

64

How exciting is it
to come to work
if the best you
can do is trounce
some other
company that
does roughly the
same thing?

LARRY PAGE
Wired, 2013

65

If change is the one thing you can be sure of, the goal is to figure out how you can use that certainty to your advantage, to modify, transfigure, refashion, and transform your day-to-day being.

OPRAH WINFREY
O, The Oprah Magazine, 2014

66

We just believe that an independent entrepreneur will always beat a division of a big company, which is why we think that the strategy of these other companies trying to do everything themselves will inevitably be less successful than an ecosystem where you have someone like Facebook trying to build the core product to help people connect and then independent great companies that are only focused on one or two things doing those things really well.

MARK ZUCKERBERG
Charlie Rose, 2011

67

Entrepreneurial business favors the open mind. It favors people whose optimism drives them to prepare for many possible futures, pretty much purely for the joy of doing so.

RICHARD BRANSON
Richard's blog, 2012

68

When you first start off trying to solve a problem, the first solutions you come up with are very complex, and most people stop there. But if you keep going, and live with the problem and peel more layers of the onion off, you can oftentimes arrive at some very elegant and simple solutions. Most people just don't put in the time or energy to get there.

STEVE JOBS
Newsweek, 2006

69

The long distance needed to reach your goal isn't the problem. The problem is not knowing just how far that distance is.

JACK MA
Ningbo Network Operators Meeting, 2002

70

Strength accumulates from failure. If someday I brag to my grandchild all about my fine achievements, he or she may simply say, "What's so great about that? You simply rode the swelling internet commerce tide in and found some investment." But if I talk about all my failures and mistakes in those years, then he or she may look at me with admiration. Final success includes many miserable experiences.

JACK MA
Ningbo Network Operators Meeting, 2002

There are three things you look for: You have to look forward in the morning to doing your work. You do want to have a significant financial reward. And you want to have a possible effect on the world. *If you can find all three, you have something you can tell your children.*

ELON MUSK
Pennsylvania Gazette, 2008

72

I am not the most talented person.
My appearance, abilities, and
education are far from society's best.
But I understand human nature.
You must control the negative
and build up the positive to attain
success. I try to do this through team
spirit and shared missions.

JACK MA
dialogue with Kazuo Inamori, 2008

73

Most all the mistakes I've
made in my life, I've made
because I was trying to please
other people.... Every mistake
I've ever made was because I
went outside of myself to do
something for somebody else
that I should not have.

———

OPRAH WINFREY
Academy of Achievement, 1991

74

Anyone can start up a new business from home. You can wash windows, take in ironing, or walk dogs. You can be an artist or a writer.... Even the Queen sells her farm produce from Windsor and Sandringham on the Web, as does Prince Charles with his Duchy Originals.

RICHARD BRANSON
Screw It, Let's Do It, 2008

75

Fundamentally, if you don't have a compelling product at a compelling price, you don't have a great company.

ELON MUSK
Inc. 5000 Conference, 2008

76

WHEN WE FACE
OUR PROBLEMS, THEY
DISAPPEAR. SO LEARN
FROM FAILURE AND
**LET SUCCESS BE THE
SILENT INCENTIVE**.

CARLOS SLIM
American University of Beirut, 2010

77

If you are talking about education at school, the marks you have—compared with the marks of others—are just qualifications. They aren't the same as your knowledge, your way of understanding the world.

CARLOS SLIM
Korn/Ferry Briefings on Talent & Leadership, 2010

78

The minimum passing grade is excellent. That's the way I believe startup companies need to be if they're ultimately going to be large and successful companies. . . . If you're going to get through a really tough environment and ultimately grow the company to something significant, you have to have a very high level of dedication and talent throughout the organization.

ELON MUSK
Web 2.0 Summit, 2008

79

There's a machismo about the way some managers talk about hiring and firing that I find downright repugnant. . . . I think that you should only fire somebody as an act of last resort.

RICHARD BRANSON
Business Stripped Bare, 2008

80

My job is not
to be easy
on people.
My job is to
make them
better.

STEVE JOBS
Fortune, 2008

81

*I believe the leader sets
the direction, and even
the emotional tone, of an
organization. It is about
satisfying the emotional needs
of people. It's not about taking
responsibility for things.*

CARLOS SLIM
Korn/Ferry Briefings on Talent & Leadership, 2010

82

I spend my
time thinking
about how
to **build** this
and not how
to **exit**.

MARK ZUCKERBERG
Entrepreneurial Thought Leaders Seminars, 2005

If you work with people who cause your stomach to churn, I'd say **get another job**. That is a terrible way to go through life, and you only go through life once.

WARREN BUFFETT
Georgia Tech Alumni Magazine, 2003

84

The way you step up your game is not to worry about the other guy in any situation, because you can't control the other guy. You only have control over yourself. So it's like running a race. The energy that it takes to look back and see where the other guys are takes energy away from you.... Don't waste your time in the race looking back to see where the other guy is or what the other guy is doing. **It's not about the other guy. It's about what can you do.**

OPRAH WINFREY
Oprah's Master Class, 2011

85

We don't think too much about
what competitors are doing
because I think it's important to
be focused on making the best
possible products. It's maybe
analogous to what they say
about if you're in a race: don't
worry about what the other
runners are doing—just run.

ELON MUSK
StartmeupHK Venture Forum, 2016

The demands and the amount of work it takes to put something like [Facebook] into place, it's just so much that if you weren't completely into what you were doing and you didn't think it was an important thing, then it would be irrational to spend that much time on it.

MARK ZUCKERBERG
Time, 2007

87

Smart people ought to be able to figure anything out if they get enough facts.

BILL GATES
Showstopper!, 1994

88

The way our ladder works, you can keep getting promoted to new levels just by being better at creating the product. **It's important to set examples.** When something works out, you take the guys involved in that project and you make them heroes. You let everyone know that people should strive to be like them.

BILL GATES
Success Magazine, 1988

89

When you're the most
successful person in
your family, in your
neighborhood and in
your town, everybody
thinks you're the First
National Bank and you
have to figure out for
yourself where those
boundaries are.

OPRAH WINFREY
The Hollywood Reporter, 2013

90

The future is never clear;
you pay a very high
price in the stock market
for a cheery consensus.
Uncertainty actually is
the friend of the buyer of
long-term values.

WARREN BUFFETT
Forbes, 1979

91

INNOVATION DISTINGUISHES BETWEEN A **LEADER** AND A **FOLLOWER**.

STEVE JOBS

The Innovation Secrets of Steve Jobs, 2011

92

*A true leader
does require three
scarce attributes:*
intelligence,
courage *and*
benevolence.
*Some leaders are
brave and smart,
yet bad-tempered
and destructive;
others are
benevolent while
lacking the two
other attributes.*

CARLOS SLIM
keynote speech at the First International Congress of Miraflores College, 2011

93

Another function of a leader is to discover the unique skills in every member of his team. In this world, **there are no bad employees, only bad leaders and bad systems**. Nurture carefully every worker's potential without exhausting it.

JACK MA
Shanghai Network Operators Meeting, 2005

94

My job as a leader
is to make sure
everybody in the
company has great
opportunities, and that
they feel they're having
a meaningful impact
and are contributing to
the good of society.

LARRY PAGE
Fortune, 2012

95

Conduct yourself
as a leader by
being farsighted,
broadminded, and
capable and by
working together
with others. This is
how I understand
what it means to be
a talented leader.

JACK MA
Lakeside Academy, 2008

A lot of people in our industry haven't had very diverse experiences. So they don't have enough dots to connect, and they end up with very linear solutions without a broad perspective on the problem. **The broader one's understanding of the human experience, the better design we will have.**

STEVE JOBS
Wired, 1996

97

I didn't have a lot of mentors,
you know? I happened into
being a businesswoman. It has
never been a goal of mine, and
I wouldn't necessarily even
say it's a strength of mine. . . .
I have to really work at it. I
have to work at disciplining
myself. **The business of the
business tires me out.**

OPRAH WINFREY
The Hollywood Reporter, 2007

98

Inflation, someone said many years ago, is an invisible tax that only one man in a million really understands. It is a tax on people that have had faith in their currency, the governments issued it. The best investment against inflation is to improve your own earning power, your own talent. Very few people maximize their talent. If you increase your talent, they can't tax it or they can't take it away from you.

WARREN BUFFETT
Forbes India, 2011

99

I'M HERE TO BUILD SOMETHING FOR THE LONG TERM. ANYTHING ELSE IS A DISTRACTION.

MARK ZUCKERBERG
Fast Company, 2007

100

I've always been hardcore about looking at what we did wrong. We're not known for reflecting back on the things that went well. We can be pretty brutal about the parts that don't do well.

BILL GATES
Masters of Enterprise, 1999

101

I have every possession
I want. I have a lot of
friends who have a lot more
possessions. But in some
cases, I feel the possession
possesses them, rather
than the other way around.

WARREN BUFFETT
CBS News, 2012

Protecting the downside is critical. We'll make bold moves, but we'll also make sure we've got ways out if things go wrong.

RICHARD BRANSON
Peter Brojde Leadership Lecture, 2010

103

If merely looking
up past financial
data would tell
you what the
future holds,
the Forbes 400
would consist of
librarians.

WARREN BUFFETT
letter to Berkshire Hathaway shareholders, 2009

104

Always keep in mind
these three principles:
what you **want** to do,
what you **should** do,
and for **how long** you
should do it.

JACK MA
Beijing Network Operators Meeting, 2008

105

I try to keep bureaucracy to a minimum, and remind my teams that business, as well as life, should be fun.

RICHARD BRANSON
Entrepreneur, 2012

106

If our mission is to make the world more open and connected, I certainly think that starts with us ourselves. We have this very open culture at the company. Every Friday afternoon, I get up and do a Q&A where anyone in the company can get up and ask me anything they want. One of the things I'm taking away from this is that if we want to lead the world and be the best service for this kind of sharing, that we should really probably be doing a lot more of it ourselves.

MARK ZUCKERBERG
Time, 2010

107

SCREW IT, JUST GET ON AND **DO** IT.

RICHARD BRANSON
National Achievers Congress, 2011

I have no secret.
There are no
rules to follow in
business. I just
work hard and, as I
always have done,
believe I can do it.

RICHARD BRANSON
Screw It, Let's Do It, 2008

109

People judge
you by your
performance,
so focus on the
outcome. Be
a yardstick of
quality. Some
people aren't
used to an
environment
where excellence
is expected.

STEVE JOBS
Steve Jobs: The Journey is the Reward, 1987

If we can't win on quality, we shouldn't win at all.

LARRY PAGE
I'm Feeling Lucky, 2011

111

Quality is more
important than
quantity. . . .
One home run is
much better than
two doubles.

STEVE JOBS
Bloomberg Businessweek, 2006

112

The challenge of life, I have found, is to build a resume that doesn't simply tell a story about what you want to be, but it's a story about **who you want to be**. It's a resume that doesn't just tell a story about what you want to accomplish, but why. A story that's not just a collection of titles and positions, but a story that's really about your purpose.

OPRAH WINFREY
commencement address at Harvard University, 2013

113

Your time is limited, so don't waste it living someone else's life. Don't be trapped by dogma—which is living with the results of other people's thinking. Don't let the noise of others' opinions drown out your own inner voice. And most important, *have the courage to follow your heart and intuition*. They somehow already know what you truly want to become. Everything else is secondary.

STEVE JOBS
commencement address at Stanford University, 2005

114

Don't let people talk you into what they think is you.

OPRAH WINFREY
The Hollywood Reporter, 2013

115

Pride is individual, internal; it is not about recognition or applause from others. It is the **internal feeling** you have for the things you do.

CARLOS SLIM
El País, 2008

116

Your life's work is
to find your life's
work—and then
to exercise the
discipline, tenacity
and hard work it
takes to pursue it.

OPRAH WINFREY
O, The Oprah Magazine, 2001

117

It sounds better in Spanish, but
I'll say it in English anyway:
**"Impose your will against
your weakness."**
That is what I believe.

CARLOS SLIM
Korn/Ferry Briefings on Talent & Leadership, 2010

118

Knowing what you **don't** want to do is the best possible place to be ... because knowing what you don't want to do leads you to figure out what it is you really **do** want to do.

OPRAH WINFREY
Stanford Graduate School of Business, 2014

119

If you look at the artists, if they get really good, it always occurs to them at some point that they can do this one thing for the rest of their lives, and they can be really successful to the outside world but not really be successful to themselves. That's the moment that an artist really decides who he or she is. **If they keep on risking failure, they're still artists.**

STEVE JOBS
Fortune, 1998

You never lose
a dream; it
just incubates
as a hobby.

LARRY PAGE
commencement address at the University of Michigan, 2009

121

Don't expect the
clarity to come all
at once, to know
your purpose
right away.

OPRAH WINFREY
commencement address at Harvard University, 2013

My goal is not to have a job. Making cool things is just something I love doing, and not having someone tell me what to do or a timeframe in which to do it is the luxury I am looking for in my life. . . . I assume eventually I'll make something that is profitable.

MARK ZUCKERBERG
Harvard Crimson, 2004

Once my life was mine
to design, I found
myself a bit unbalanced
in structuring it. I've had
to learn to **plan what
I want to do** instead
of always fulfilling the
"have to dos."

OPRAH WINFREY
O, The Oprah Magazine, 2015

124

There become a few magic moments where you have to have confidence in yourself....When I dropped out of Harvard and said to my friends, "Come work for me," there was a certain kind of brass self-confidence in that. You have a few moments like that where trusting yourself and saying yes, this can come together—you have to seize on those because not many come along.

BILL GATES
CNBC town hall meeting, 2009

125

WHAT'S THE
SMARTEST THING
TO DO AFTER
LEARNING WHAT
MAKES YOU TICK?
**ANSWER: WASTE
ZERO TIME GETTING
STARTED ON LIVING
YOUR BEST LIFE.**

OPRAH WINFREY
O, The Oprah Magazine, 2015

126

Your best investment is yourself.

There is nothing that compares to it.

WARREN BUFFETT
Georgia Tech Alumni Magazine, 2003

127

You understand that when you know better, you ought to do better—and **doing better sometimes means changing your mind**; and you realize that letting go of what others think you should do is the only way to reach your full potential.

OPRAH WINFREY
O, The Oprah Magazine, 2001

I think the best place to learn ethics is in the home. I think most of us get our values from what we see around us before we get to business school. I think that it's important to emphasize them, but I think that if I had a choice of having great education and ethics fully on in the home or as a course in a school later on, I would choose the home.

WARREN BUFFETT
CNBC town hall meeting, 2009

129

When I first
started being a
"businesswoman,"
I worried about,
"How do you
do this?" And I
realized that you do
this the same way
as you do anything
else. **You be fair.**
You try to be
honest with other
people, and be fair.

OPRAH WINFREY
Academy of Achievement, 1991

130

The biggest lesson I got is
the power of unconditional
love. If you offer that to
your child you're 90 percent
of the way home. If every
parent out there can extend
that to their child at a very
young age—it's going to make
for a better human being.

WARREN BUFFETT
The Huffington Post, 2010

131

Fortitude and emotional balance are part of your inner self and are achieved by avoiding negative feelings such as envy, jealousy, arrogance, egoism, and greed, feelings that are a poison which is ingested bit by bit.

CARLOS SLIM
commencement address at George Washington University, 2012

132

I was lucky enough to get the right foundation very early on. And then basically I didn't listen to anybody else. I just look in the mirror every morning and the mirror always agrees with me.

WARREN BUFFETT
CNBC town hall meeting, 2009

133

Do not allow negative feelings and emotions to control your mind. Emotional harm does not come from others; it is conceived and developed within ourselves.

CARLOS SLIM
Carlosslim.com, 1994

134

I think at some point it is appropriate to stand up for your principles, and if more companies, governments, [and] individuals did that, I do think the world would be a better place.

SERGEY BRIN
Sergey Brin and Larry Page, 2010

135

Act always
as your
conscience
dictates,
because it
never lies.

———————

CARLOS SLIM
Carlosslim.com, 1994

136

Be firm in your beliefs.
Hold on to them, study
them, and do the right
thing by them. These
four key points guided
Alibaba's early steps.
Without this faith, you
cannot walk.

JACK MA
Hangzhou Network Operators Meeting, 2007

137

Do you have the right axioms, are they relevant, and are you making the right conclusions based on those axioms? That's the essence of criticial thinking, and yet it is amazing how often people fail to do that. I think wishful thinking is innate in the human brain. You want things to be the way you wish them to be, and so you tend to filter information that you shouldn't filter.

ELON MUSK
CLEAN-tech Investor Summit, 2011

138

As for "Don't be evil," we have tried to define precisely what it means to be a force for good— always to do the right, ethical thing. Ultimately, "Don't be evil" seems the easiest way to summarize it . . . [But] [i]t's not enough not to be evil. **We also actively try to be good.**

SERGEY BRIN
Playboy, 2004

139

The decisions we've made along the way reflect that, really, we always try to do the right thing. We really care about that. When we make mistakes, it's just because we were being foolish or stupid or whatever, but it's really always made with the right motivations. We say the things that we believe even when sometimes those things we believe are delusional.

ELON MUSK
Tesla Annual Shareholders Meeting, 2016

140

I think the *artistry is in having an insight into what one sees around them*—generally putting things together in a way no one else has before and finding a way to express that to other people who don't have that insight.

STEVE JOBS
Smithsonian Institution Oral and Video Histories, 1995

141

I think most people can learn a lot more than they think they can. They sell themselves short without trying. One bit of advice: it is important to view knowledge as sort of a semantic tree—make sure you understand the fundamental principles, i.e., the trunk and big branches, before you get into the leaves/details or there is nothing for them to hang on to.

ELON MUSK
Reddit AMA, 2015

142

YOU DON'T NEED
TO TAKE NOTES.
IF IT'S IMPORTANT,
**YOU'LL REMEMBER
IT.**

STEVE JOBS
Inside Steve's Brain, 2009

It shouldn't be that you've got these grades where people move in lockstep and everyone goes through English, math, science, and so forth from fifth grade to sixth grade to seventh grade like it's an assembly line. **People are not objects on an assembly line.** That's a ridiculous notion. People learn and are interested in different things at different paces.

ELON MUSK
SXSW Conference, 2013

144

As a leader, a CEO's education must include getting out to see the world and thinking about what he observes.... This is the way to bring opportunity and fortune to clients.

JACK MA
Hangzhou Network Operators Meeting, 2007

145

One of the other big lessons that I've learned, particularly in business, is that you have a responsibility to yourself to learn as much about your business as you can.

OPRAH WINFREY
Academy of Achievement, 1991

146

I care a lot about the truth of things and trying to understand the truth of things. I think that's important. If you're going to come up with some solution, then the truth is really, really important.

ELON MUSK
AutoBild.tv, 2014

147

I would trade all of my technology for an afternoon with Socrates.

STEVE JOBS
Newsweek, 2001

148

I began scheduling little moments of calm—moments in which I do nothing for at least ten minutes. . . . Whenever I give myself these little breaks, I find I have more energy, and I'm in a better mood for all the business that comes afterward.

OPRAH WINFREY
What I Know For Sure, 2014

149

Live … with intelligence,
with soul and senses aware
and on the alert; get to
know their manifestations
and **train yourselves to
appreciate and enjoy life**.

CARLOS SLIM
Carlosslim.com, 1994

150

I think I'm good at inventing
solutions to problems.
Things seem fairly obvious
to me that are clearly not
obvious to most people. And
I'm not really trying to do it
or anything. It just seems like
I see the truth of things and
others seem less able to do so.

ELON MUSK
Morning Edition, 2007

Smartness is an ability to absorb new facts.
To walk into a situation, have something explained to you, and immediately say, "Well, what about this?" To ask an insightful question. To absorb it in real time. A capacity to remember. To relate to domains that may not seem connected at first.

BILL GATES
The Rich and How They Got That Way, 2001

152

People must have time to think about things.

BILL GATES
Advertising Age, 1996

153

The ability to listen, and
the willingness to stick
your neck out and ask
the obvious question,
are criminally underrated
business essentials.

RICHARD BRANSON
Business Stripped Bare, 2008

We should aspire to increase
the scope and scale of
human consciousness in
order to better understand
what questions to ask.
Really, the only thing that
makes sense is to strive
for greater collective
enlightenment.

ELON MUSK
Bloomberg, 2012

155

The best way
to think about
investments
is to be in a
room with no
one else and
to just think.
If that doesn't
work, nothing
else is going
to work.

WARREN BUFFETT
colloquium at the University of Florida, 1998

156

Pay attention to your own development and keep learning constantly. Never blame God or others for your position in life. Blame yourself.

JACK MA
Shanghai Network Operators Meeting, 2005

157

You can learn whatever you need to do to start a successful business either in school or out of school. A school, in theory, should help accelerate that process, and I think oftentimes it does.... the important principle is to be dedicated to learning what you need to know, whether that is in school or empirically.

ELON MUSK
lecture at Stanford University, 2003

158

Arming myself with
knowledge and sitting down
with people who live the topic
and brainstorming with them,
that's what helps me back the
right people and make sure I
know what's going on.

BILL GATES
CNBC town hall meeting, 2009

159

Business requires astute decision-making and leadership. It requires discipline and innovation. It also needs attitude, a good sense of humor, and, dare I say it, *luck*.

RICHARD BRANSON
Business Stripped Bare, 2008

160

I don't think that
IQ is as fungible
as I used to. To
succeed, you also
have to know how
to make choices
and how to think
more broadly.

BILL GATES
Time, 1997

161

The day you become a leader, you will be very lonely. Even the second- and third-in-command will find it difficult to understand you well. When the captain sets sail, sometimes he personally climbs up the ship's pole to see which way the wind is blowing. For myself, I need to think of things a year ahead of time, to consider the right systems and deployment of human resources to come. Success may be another year off, so decisions now may not be clear until then.

JACK MA
Shenzhen Network Operators Meeting, 2008

162

I think the CEO
basically does two
things: They set
the **vision** for the
company, and they
recruit a team.

MARK ZUCKERBERG
D6 Conference, 2008

163

All companies start small and grow. . . . But as the businesses grow, sometimes the founder is no longer the best person to run the company. Then, you need to find the best people to run the business. You need to find the best executives—people who do that particular job very well. I say this because the CEO is very important to the success of the organization.

CARLOS SLIM
Korn/Ferry Briefings on Talent & Leadership, 2010

164

As a small-business person, you must immerse yourself 100 percent in everything and learn about the ins and outs of every single department.... And as the business gets bigger, you will have to decide if you're a **manager** or an **entrepreneur**. If you're a manager you can stay with that business and help it grow. If you're an entrepreneur, you need to find a manager. Then you should move on, enjoy yourself and then set up your next enterprise.

RICHARD BRANSON
Business Stripped Bare, 2008

165

Control of a company should never be about the number of shares a CEO holds. Rather, it should be about his or her wisdom and vision. Build your organization with a scientific, rational management team and *don't allow any single investor or person full control*.

JACK MA
Fortune Life Program, 2003

166

As a company, if you can just get those two things right—having a clear direction on what you are trying to do, and bringing in great people who can execute on the stuff—then you can do pretty well.

MARK ZUCKERBERG
D8 Conference, 2010

167

For as much as you need a strong personality to build a business from scratch, you must also understand the **art of delegation**. I have to be willing to step back now. I have to be good at helping people run the individual businesses—it can't just be me that sets the culture when we recruit people.

RICHARD BRANSON
HR, 2010

168

I don't have to be smart about everything; I didn't deliver my wife's baby! So, I believe in using people who are smarter than I am.

WARREN BUFFETT
Forbes India, 2011

I TRY TO SURROUND MYSELF WITH PEOPLE WHO REALLY KNOW WHAT THEY'RE DOING AND [THEN] **GIVE THEM THE FREEDOM TO DO IT**.

OPRAH WINFREY
Fast Company, 2015

170

It's not just recruiting.
After recruiting, it's then
building an environment
that makes people feel
they are surrounded by
equally talented people
and that their work is
bigger than they are.

STEVE JOBS
In the Company of Giants, 1997

171

Our system does
not rely on one
or two people. If
I leave and the
company collapses,
then it wasn't well
constructed.

JACK MA
APEC 5th e-Business Champions Grand Awards Ceremony, 2008

All we are is our ideas, or people. That's what keeps us going to work in the morning, to hang around these great bright people. I've always thought that recruiting is the heart and soul of what we do.

STEVE JOBS
D5 Conference, 2007

We don't hire because we get a tax break or because someone in the government tells us to. We hire when there's more demand for what we are making or moving or selling. It's that simple.

WARREN BUFFETT
Fortune, 2010

174

The people who are doing the work are the moving force behind the Macintosh. My job is to create a space for them, to clear out the rest of the organization and keep it at bay. . . . This is the neatest group of people I've ever worked with. They're all exceptionally bright, but more importantly they share a quality about the way they look at life, which is that the journey is the reward.

STEVE JOBS
Macworld, 1984

175

The biggest mistake in general that I've made—and I'm trying to correct for that—is to put too much of a weighting on somebody's talent and not enough on their personality.... **It actually matters whether somebody has a good heart.** It really does. And I've made the mistake of thinking that sometimes it's just about the brain.

ELON MUSK
SXSW Conference, 2013

176

I used to do for every employee—now I have 700, so I can't—but I used to do what I call "the gut check." I would just spend a few minutes doing my own emotional check of how I felt about this person, whether I sensed their honesty.

OPRAH WINFREY
The Hollywood Reporter, 2007

177

From a young age, if I ever criticized somebody, my parents would make me go and stand in front of the mirror, and they just said, "Look, it's a bad reflection on yourself." Ever since then, in particular if you're running a company, you've just got to look for the best in everybody. . . . **I think if you deal well with people, people will come back and deal with you again.**

RICHARD BRANSON
National Achievers Congress, 2011

178

By far, the most important quality is not how much IQ you've got. IQ is not the scarce factor. You need a reasonable amount of intelligence, but the **temperament** is 90 percent of it.

WARREN BUFFETT
lecture at the University of Notre Dame, 1991

Four qualities
are needed along
with talent:
trustworthiness,
team spirit,
adaptability, and
optimism.

JACK MA
First Financial Daily, 2005

Titles aren't important.

We'll all do better if we

have a flat organization

with few levels to facilitate

communication and avoid

bureaucracy.

SERGEY BRIN
I'm Feeling Lucky, 2011

181

We focus on operation. We take down as many [management] levels as we can, to make the highest level be near the operation. With practice and experience, we make a team that's very efficient, and we do that very fast.

CARLOS SLIM
Academy of Achievement, 2007

We have a business with very few rules. **The only rules the managers have is to basically think like owners.** We want those people thinking exactly like they own those businesses themselves. Psychologically, we don't even want them to think there is a Berkshire Hathaway.

WARREN BUFFETT
lecture at the University of Notre Dame, 1991

183

We're very big on managers who are very much in touch with doing hands-on work, who appreciate the work that people underneath them are doing, and retain the skill sets to jump in and do some of it themselves. So they can understand what is the load like, what's hard, how's that going on, and pitch in when there is something that's particularly tough.

BILL GATES
keynote speech at San Jose State, 1998

184

An investor, a speculator, can do it by himself. Well, nearly by himself. He needs information but he can do it without any people, with a small office. But if you're operating a business, if you're operating companies, if you're operating industries, **you need a team to make it happen**. Always look to make it better, and as long as you have a good team, you can do that.

CARLOS SLIM
Academy of Achievement, 2007

I've never done anything solo, except take tests.

BILL GATES
Working Together, 2010

My model for business is the Beatles. They were four very talented guys who kept each other's kind of negative tendencies in check. They balanced each other and the total was greater than the sum of the parts. That's how I see business: great things in business are never done by one person, they're done by a team of people.

STEVE JOBS
60 Minutes, 2008

187

A company's identity is somewhat similar to a zoo's. Just as a zoo is enhanced by having a wide variety of animals, so too does a company benefit from a talented staff representing all walks of life. This can only aid in innovation.

JACK MA
"Lakeside Talk," 2007

188

I love bees because I think that the beehive is a metaphor for the world. Every member of the community is of equal value, although they have different tasks.

RICHARD BRANSON
Screw Business As Usual, 2011

189

In terms of doing
work and in terms
of learning and
evolving as a person,
you just grow more
when you get more
people's perspectives.

MARK ZUCKERBERG
Charlie Rose, 2011

190

There was a great sense of teamwork within our family. Whenever we were within Mum's orbit, we had to be busy. If we tried to escape by saying that we had something else to do, we were firmly told we were selfish. As a result, we grew up with a clear priority of putting other people first.

RICHARD BRANSON
Losing My Virginity, 1988

191

It's important that the company be a family, that people feel that they're part of the company, and that the company is like a family to them. When you treat people that way, you get better productivity. Rather than caring what hours you worked, you care about output. We should continue to innovate in our relationship with our employees and figure out the best things we can do for them.

LARRY PAGE
Fortune, 2012

Hire the person **best suited to the job**, not the most talented. This can be a very painful lesson. There's no point putting in a Boeing jet engine when you need to run a tractor.

JACK MA
Dongguan Network Operators Meeting, 2005

193

I think it's a bad decision
to give a child a great job
simply because he is your
child, and I don't like it
when someone places too
much pressure or over-
expects from them because
they are your child. You
must find the job that goes
with their strength, their
talents, their personality,
pleasure and drive.
Otherwise no one wins.

CARLOS SLIM
Carlos Slim: The Richest Man in the World, 2013

194

A SMALL GROUP
OF VERY
TECHNICALLY
STRONG
PEOPLE WILL
ALWAYS BEAT
A LARGE
GROUP OF
MODERATELY
STRONG
PEOPLE.

ELON MUSK
Fast Company, 2005

195

You can't just get a
bunch of smart people
together and know
which path they should
go off and pursue.
Actually, it's amazing
that that worked for
the Manhattan Project.

BILL GATES
Technology Review, 2010

196

When I go to a meeting, I keep specific objectives in mind. There isn't much small talk, especially if I'm with colleagues I know well. We discuss accounts we lost or where overhead is too high, and then we're done. Bang! There are always more challenges than there are hours, so why be wasteful?

BILL GATES
New York Times, 1996

197

When we first started having our board meetings a few years back what I'd do is just start writing down a summary of what was going on with the business on a yellow piece of paper and give it to the board, and we used to have these really focused, great discussions of what was going on. Since then the board meetings have gotten a bit more structured: there's a bit more information handed out. But at the end of all the meetings our directors just say, "You know, I still love that single piece of paper with a summary of what's going on."

———————

MARK ZUCKERBERG
Fast Company: 30 Second MBA

198

We want to make sure that everyone can come and add their ideas. I mean, some of the best ideas throughout the company's evolution, they have just been from just places all throughout the company, whether it's an engineer or someone on the customer support team.

MARK ZUCKERBERG
Business Insider, 2010

199

Smart people anywhere in the company should have the power to drive an initiative.

BILL GATES
Business @ the Speed of Thought, 1999

200

Empowering employees so that they can make good decisions is one of an entrepreneur's most important tasks. This means that you must build a corporate comfort zone in which your people can confidently express themselves and display the courage of their own convictions.

RICHARD BRANSON
Like a Virgin, 2012

201

This is where you want to make sure you are hiring employees because they love to work here, they love to create things, and they're not here primarily for the money. Although when they do create something valuable you want to reward them. That's when these things really pay off. I like to think we're putting a lot of investment in things that matter a lot more when you're not having such a great time as a company.

SERGEY BRIN
Fortune, 2008

202

Not everybody is cut out to be an entrepreneur. But that doesn't mean you can't still come up with new ideas working within an organization. This is where **intrapreneurs** come in: They unleash the power of innovation from inside companies.

RICHARD BRANSON
Richard's blog, 2012

203

We do try to attract people, but our goal isn't necessarily to keep people forever. . . . If you want to build a company, nothing's better than jumping in and trying to build one. But Facebook is also great for entrepreneurs/hackers. If people want to come for a few years and move on and build something great, that's something we're proud of.

MARK ZUCKERBERG
Startup School, 2011

204

Groups cannot compete against each other inside the company. We need to go in the same direction— not competing on the inside but competing on the outside.

CARLOS SLIM
No Fear of Failure, 2011

205

Building a company
is one of the most
efficient ways in the
world that you can
kind of align the
incentives of a lot of
smart people towards
making a change.

MARK ZUCKERBERG
Startup School, 2011

206

One of the interesting things we noticed was that companies correlate on decision-making and speed of decision-making. There are basically no companies that have good slow decisions. There are only companies that have good fast decisions. So I think that's also a natural thing: As companies get bigger, they tend to slow down decision-making. **And that's pretty tragic.**

LARRY PAGE
Zeitgeist, 2011

When we decide to do something, we do it quickly.

CARLOS SLIM
Bloomberg Businessweek, 2005

208

The heaviness of being successful was replaced by the lightness of being a beginner again, less sure about everything. It freed me to enter one of the most creative periods of my life.

STEVE JOBS
commencement address at Stanford University, 2005

209

Live without fears and without guilt. Fear is the worst sentiment of human beings. It weakens us, inhibits actions, and depresses us. Guilt is a tremendous burden that weighs down our thinking, our actions, and our lives. **Fear and guilt make the present difficult and obstruct the future.**

CARLOS SLIM
commencement address at George Washington University, 2012

210

There's no map.
By its nature, it's
unknown, which
means you're going
to make false moves.
It must be OK to
make false moves.

ELON MUSK
Boao Forum for Asia, 2015

As long as human beings run institutions, including financial institutions, there will be people that take undue risks, there will sometimes be people that steal, there will be—you know, there will be people that don't understand the risks they're taking. It's just the nature of business.

WARREN BUFFETT
Squawk Box, 2011

212

I believe that uncertainty is my spirit's way of whispering, *I'm in flux. I can't decide for you. Something is off balance here.* I take that as a cue to re-center myself before making a decision.

OPRAH WINFREY
What I Know For Sure, 2014

[Have] a really strong sense of what you want to do, because along the way there are so many distractions that if you're not completely clear on what you want to do, you're going to get sidetracked.

MARK ZUCKERBERG

Computer History Museum, 2010

214

Life is always
speaking to us,
especially in our
greatest trials.
The question is
will you listen
to the whispers.

OPRAH WINFREY
Ebony, 2014

Don't make the same decision twice. Spend time and thought to make a solid decision the first time so that you don't revisit the issue unnecessarily. . . . After all, why bother deciding an issue if it isn't really decided?

BILL GATES
New York Times, 1997

216

A simple rule dictates my buying: Be fearful when others are greedy, and be greedy when others are fearful.

WARREN BUFFETT
New York Times, 2008

217

Whomever doesn't invest for any reason, out of fear, precaution or whatever, will stay behind.

CARLOS SLIM
Agence France-Presse, 2011

218

All success comes

with patience, and

with patience

comes power.

OPRAH WINFREY
The Hollywood Reporter, 2012

219

FIRM AND
PATIENT
OPTIMISM
ALWAYS
YIELDS ITS
REWARDS.

CARLOS SLIM
Carlosslim.com, 2007

220

How do you know
whether you're on
the right path, with
the right person,
or in the right job?
The same way you
know when you're
not. **You feel it.**

OPRAH WINFREY
O, The Oprah Magazine, 2001

221

Chronic pessimism leads ... to mediocrity.

CARLOS SLIM
commencement address at George Washington University, 2012

222

I don't waste much time ruing the past. I made my decision, and the way to do it best is, once you make it, you just don't waver at all. . . . Being hard-core and forward looking about what you do is a necessary element of doing it well.

BILL GATES
Forbes ASAP, 1994

223

I have from the very beginning listened to my instinct. All of my best decisions in life have come because I was attuned to what really felt like the next right move for me.

OPRAH WINFREY
Stanford Graduate School of Business, 2014

Success is a lousy teacher. It seduces smart people into thinking they can't lose.

BILL GATES
The Road Ahead, 1995

225

ALL BUSINESSES
MAKE MISTAKES.
THE TRICK IS TO
**AVOID LARGE
ONES**.

CARLOS SLIM
Institutional Investor, 2003

226

Mistakes don't bother me. I try to never do anything that would jeopardize the well-being of the whole place. So I build into the decisions I make the fact that I am going to make mistakes.

WARREN BUFFETT
Haaretz, 2011

227

Mistakes are normal
and human. Make
them small, accept
them, correct them,
and forget them.

CARLOS SLIM
American University of Beirut, 2010

228

Start somewhere
and then really
be prepared to
**question your
assumptions**,
fix what you did
wrong, and adapt
to reality.

ELON MUSK
Vanity Fair New Establishment Summit, 2015

229

I prefer studying the reasons why businesses fail rather than why they succeed. People say that Jack Ma's leadership is the reason for Alibaba's survival. That's incorrect. I'm not that smart, but I am good at learning from experience.

JACK MA
Guangzhou Network Operators Meeting, 2005

230

Long ago, Sir Isaac Newton gave us three laws of motion, which were the work of genius. But Sir Isaac's talents didn't extend to investing: He lost a bundle in the South Sea Bubble, explaining later, "I can calculate the movement of the stars, but not the madness of men." If he had not been traumatized by this loss, Sir Isaac might well have gone on to discover the Fourth Law of Motion: *For investors as a whole, returns decrease as motion increases.*

WARREN BUFFETT
letter to Berkshire Hathaway shareholders, 2006

231

If you're in business, you
need to understand the
environment. You need
to have a vision of the
future, and for that you
need to know the past.
That is very important.

CARLOS SLIM
Academy of Achievement, 2007

232

Credit is like oxygen. When either is abundant, its presence goes unnoticed. When either is missing, that's all that is noticed. Even a short absence of credit can bring a company to its knees.

———

WARREN BUFFETT
letter to Berkshire Hathaway shareholders, 2011

233

If you only regret the fact you failed but not the reasons for it, you'll always be in a state of regret.

JACK MA
Jack Ma's Quotations on Entrepreneurship, 2008

234

You only learn who has been swimming naked when the tide goes out.

WARREN BUFFETT
letter to Berkshire Hathaway shareholders, 2008

235

LIFE IS TOO SHORT FOR LONG-TERM GRUDGES.

ELON MUSK
Inc., 2007

236

While it can be painful
today and even more painful
tomorrow, it can be beautiful
the day after tomorrow.
Keep on and hold on and
always be ready for the worst
that may happen tomorrow.
Then you'll get to see the sun
rise the day after tomorrow.

JACK MA
press conference, 2007

237

We never look
back. You know, we
just figure there's
so much to look
forward to, there's
no sense thinking
about what we might
have—it just doesn't
make any difference.
I mean, you can only
live life forward.

WARREN BUFFETT
colloquium at the University of Florida, 1998

238

That's why I think death is the most wonderful invention of life. It purges the system of these old models that are obsolete. I think that's one of Apple's challenges, really. When two young people walk in with the next thing, are we going to embrace it and say this is fantastic? Are we going to be willing to drop our models, or are we going to explain it away? I think we'll do better, because we're completely aware of it and we make it a priority.

STEVE JOBS
Playboy, 1985

Should you find yourself in a chronically leaking boat, energy devoted to changing vessels is likely to be more productive than energy devoted to patching leaks.

WARREN BUFFETT
The Essays of Warren Buffett, 1997

240

So, since becoming CEO
again, I've pushed hard to
increase our velocity, improve
our execution, and focus on
the big bets that will make
a difference in the world.
Google is a large company
now, but we will achieve
more, and do it faster, if
we approach life with the
passion and soul of a startup.

LARRY PAGE
"2012 Update from the CEO," 2012

241

We never waste a lot of time talking about what we're doing well. It just isn't our culture. Every meeting is about "Sure, we won in seven of the categories, but what about that eighth category?"

BILL GATES
Newsweek, 1996

242

When I was a student at the University of Michigan, I went on a summer leadership course. The slogan was **"A healthy disregard for the impossible,"** and it's an idea that has stayed with me ever since.... We've also found that "failed" ambitious projects often yield other dividends.

LARRY PAGE
"2012 Update from the CEO," 2012

If you want to live
your life in a creative
way, as an artist, you
have to not look back
too much. You have
to be willing to take
whatever you've done
and whoever you were
and throw them away.

STEVE JOBS
Playboy, 1985

244

What I thought, really, was that we'd lost the will to explore, that we'd lost the will to push the boundary, and in retrospect, that was actually a very foolish error. Because the United States is a nation of explorers. The United States is a distillation of the human spirit of exploration.... But people need to believe that it's possible and that it's not going to bankrupt them.

ELON MUSK
SXSW Conference, 2013

245

Entrepreneurship is also about excellence. Not excellence measured in awards or other people's approval, but the sort that one achieves for oneself by exploring what the world has to offer.

RICHARD BRANSON
Success, 2009

246

If we have a strength,
it is in recognizing
when we are operating
well within our
circle of competence
and when we are
approaching the
perimeter.

WARREN BUFFETT
letter to Berkshire Hathaway shareholders, 2000

Focus is incredibly important. If you have a certain amount of resources, to the degree that you diffuse your focus, you impede your ability to execute.

ELON MUSK
Tesla Annual Shareholders Meeting, 2016

248

As a company we're very focused on what we're building and not as focused on the exit. We just believe that we're adding a certain amount of value to people's lives if we build a very good product.

MARK ZUCKERBERG
Time, 2007

We cherish cost-consciousness at Berkshire. Our model is the widow who went to the local newspaper to place an obituary notice. Told there was a 25-cents-a-word charge, she requested "Fred Brown died." She was then informed there was a seven-word minimum. "Okay," the bereaved woman replied, "make it 'Fred Brown died, golf clubs for sale.'"

WARREN BUFFETT
letter to Berkshire Hathaway shareholders, 2003

250

I devote maybe ten percent to business thinking. **Business isn't that complicated.** I wouldn't want to put it on my business card. [I'm a] scientist. Unless I've been fooling myself. When I read about great scientists like, say, Crick and Watson and how they discovered DNA, I get a lot of pleasure. Stories of business success don't interest me in the same way. Say you added two years to my life and let me go to business school. I don't think I would have done a better job at Microsoft.

BILL GATES
Playboy, 1994

251

I don't think
of myself as a
businessperson. . . .
I don't think that
I've focused on a lot
of the same things
that a lot of other
businesspeople
do, but every day
we try to come in
and build the best
product for people.

MARK ZUCKERBERG
Time, 2010

252

No matter what, you must
have a dream. This is
the best working capital
to start with. Second,
keep at it. There may be
smarter people and more
industrious people, but why
did we succeed and make
money when others didn't?
We kept at it.

JACK MA
Hangzhou Network Operators Meeting, 2007

253

Life has to be about more than solving problems. If all that life is about is solving problems, why bother getting up in the morning? There have to be things that inspire you, that make you proud to be a member of humanity.

ELON MUSK
press conference, 2011

It's amazing how strong a message is hidden in words like "diversity" or the broad term "corporate social responsibility." A company needs to have core values of who they are and what they do [which] makes employees feel they have a purpose and guides their action.

BILL GATES
Creative Capitalism, 2008

255

I think if you can explain the "why" of things, then that makes a huge difference to people's motivation. Then they understand purpose.

ELON MUSK
Khan Academy Chats, 2013

256

It's very important for leaders
in business to work to create
human capital that way, to give a
sense of purpose to a team, and
to the people in the organization.
If leaders do this, then people
working in organizations will
feel they are doing something
important for society and for the
people around them. They will
have a real sense of achievement.

CARLOS SLIM
Korn/Ferry Briefings on Talent & Leadership, 2010

257

We've always been significantly smaller per employee compared to the number of people who we serve in the world. So it's really baked into the company that we have to build systems and software that take into account the leverage that employees here have.

MARK ZUCKERBERG
Facebook Q2 results-earnings call, 2012

258

Whatever this thing is that you're trying to create, what would be the utility delta compared to the current state of the art times how many people it would affect? That's why I think having something that makes a big difference but affects a small to moderate number of people is great, as is something that makes even a small difference but affects a vast number of people.

ELON MUSK
Y Combinator's "How to Build the Future" series, 2016

259

Serving our end users is at the heart of what we do and remains our number one priority. Our goal is to develop services that significantly improve the lives of as many people as possible.

LARRY PAGE AND SERGEY BRIN
Amendment 9 to Form S-1, 2004

260

When you're a carpenter making a beautiful chest of drawers, you're not going to use a piece of plywood on the back, even though it faces the wall and nobody will ever see it. You'll know it's there, so you're going to use a beautiful piece of wood on the back. For you to sleep well at night, **the aesthetic, the quality, has to be carried all the way through**.

STEVE JOBS
Playboy, 1985

261

I'm a big believer in: don't ask investors to invest their money if you're not prepared to invest your money.

ELON MUSK
Tesla Annual Shareholders Meeting, 2016

262

If a bank or other investor is looking at your business, they have almost certainly looked at your competitors as well. In your presentation, therefore, it's imperative that you understand your competition and irreverently explain **why your business will do better**. Blow them away! Avoid being overly negative.

RICHARD BRANSON
Like a Virgin, 2012

263

Start with clarity
of intention.
Know yours and
your opponent's.
Make every
deal a win-win.
Otherwise, you
lose long term.

OPRAH WINFREY
The Hollywood Reporter, 2015

264

WE WEREN'T GOING TO BE THE FIRST TO THIS PARTY, BUT WE'RE GOING TO BE **THE BEST**.

STEVE JOBS
Apple event for iPhone OS 4.0, 2010

265

We don't generally talk about our strategy . . . because it's strategic. I would rather have people think we're confused than let our competitors know what we're going to do.

LARRY PAGE
Time, 2006

266

Never envy
another big
company. Your
current company
is the best as
long as you share
common goals,
missions, and
values.

JACK MA
Shanghai Network Operators Meeting, 2005

All good capitalistic companies get up every morning and think, "How can we make a better product? What are they doing well? We're going to make it cheaper, better, simpler, faster." And great competitors spur companies on. And at every phase of our industry, it's been a different set of companies.

BILL GATES
Global Public Square, 2008

268

In some ways we have run the company as to let 1,000 flowers bloom, but once they do bloom you want to put together a coherent bouquet.

SERGEY BRIN
Web 2.0 Summit, 2011

269

I don't really know what the next big thing is because I don't spend my time making big things. I spend time making small things and then when the time comes I put them together.

MARK ZUCKERBERG
Harvard Crimson, 2004

270

Bad ideas are OK.
We're not afraid of
bad ideas as much
as having no ideas.
Never be afraid
of taking quick
action to solve
current and future
problems.

JACK MA
ICBU Mobilization Meeting, 2007

Great organizations demand a high level of commitment by the people involved. That's true in any endeavor. I've never criticized a person. I have criticized ideas. If I think something's a waste of time or inappropriate I don't wait to point it out. I say it right away. It's real time. So you might hear me say, That's the dumbest idea I have ever heard many times during a meeting.

BILL GATES
Playboy, 1994

272

People think focus means saying yes to the thing you've got to focus on. But that's not what it means at all. It means saying no to the hundred other good ideas that there are. You have to pick carefully. **I'm actually as proud of the things we haven't done as the things we have done.**

STEVE JOBS
Fortune, 2008

273

My colleagues
know me as
Dr. Yes because
I find it hard
to say no to
new ideas and
proposals.

RICHARD BRANSON
Guardian, 2010

274

Don't pass up something that's attractive today because you think you will find something way more attractive tomorrow.

WARREN BUFFETT
CNBC town hall meeting, 2009

275

My whole career has been based on being truthful in the moment. And if I have to pretend to be interested in something that I'm not interested in, it doesn't work.

OPRAH WINFREY
The Hollywood Reporter, 2007

276

Always solicit critical feedback, particularly from friends. Because, generally, they will be thinking it, but they won't tell you.

ELON MUSK
SXSW Conference, 2013

277

Beware the glib helper who fills your head with fantasies while he fills his pockets with fees.

WARREN BUFFETT
letter to Berkshire Hathaway shareholders, 2008

278

When you run a business, you need to be able to laugh, too. A strong vision and active mind allows for this. Take pride in what you do, and be capable and strong. To be able to laugh and be proud requires sharp eyes and a broad mind.

JACK MA
Ningbo Network Operators Meeting, 2002

279

Live the present **fully** and **intentionally**. Let the past not be a burden. May the future be an incentive. Live with a sense of urgency when you are creating, when you are innovating, when you are solving problems, when you are building.

CARLOS SLIM
commencement address at George Washington University, 2012

280

I think
entrepreneurship
is our natural
state—a big adult
word that probably
boils down to
something much
more obvious like
"playfulness."

RICHARD BRANSON
Business Stripped Bare, 2008

281

I think if you do something and it turns out pretty good, then you should go do something else wonderful, not dwell on it for too long. **Just figure out what's next.**

STEVE JOBS

NBC Nightly News with Brian Williams, 2006

282

The most important thing that we should be doing as a business is **prioritizing**, figuring out what the right things are for us to be approaching now. . . . Working on stuff that's really important now is always like the best use of our time.

MARK ZUCKERBERG
Entrepreneurial Thought Leaders Seminars, 2005

283

We have always
tried to concentrate
on the long term,
and to place bets
on technology we
believe will have a
significant impact
over time.

LARRY PAGE
"2012 Update from the CEO," 2012

284

Degree of difficulty counts in the Olympics; it doesn't count in business. You don't get any extra points for the fact that something's very hard to do, so you might as well step over one-foot bars rather than try to jump over seven-foot bars.

WARREN BUFFETT
CNBC, 2010

285

I think a simple rule of business is, if you do the things that are easier first, then you can actually make a lot of progress.

MARK ZUCKERBERG
Charlie Rose, 2011

286

PEOPLE
UNDERESTIMATE
HOW EFFECTIVE
CAPITALISM IS
AT KEEPING
EVEN THE MOST
SUCCESSFUL
COMPANIES ON
EDGE.

BILL GATES
The Rich and How They Got That Way, 2001

287

It's often easier to make progress when you're really ambitious. And the reason is that you actually don't have any competition because no one is willing to try those things. . . . ***Anything you can imagine probably is doable.*** You just have to imagine it and work on it.

LARRY PAGE
Zeitgeist, 2012

288

For the core things that we wanna do, when we have the decision to either do it the same way that someone else has done it or do it a different way, we're gonna choose to do it in a different way. And we really encourage people all throughout the company to think about things in that way and make bolder decisions.

MARK ZUCKERBERG
Business Insider, 2010

289

It's more fun to be a pirate than to join the Navy.

STEVE JOBS
Odyssey: Pepsi to Apple, 1987

290

Ultimately, it comes down to taste. It comes down to trying to expose yourself to the best things that humans have done and then try to bring those things in to what you're doing. . . . Picasso had a saying: good artists copy, great artists steal. And we have always been shameless about stealing great ideas.

STEVE JOBS
Triumph of the Nerds, 1996

291

Through most of our life, we get through life by reasoning by analogy, which essentially means kind of copying what other people do with slight variations. But when you want to do something new, you have to apply the physics [first principles] approach. Physics has really figured out how to discover new things that are counterintuitive, like quantum mechanics.

ELON MUSK
TED Talk, 2013

292

You have to be a little silly about the goals you are going to set. . . . You should try to do things most people would not.

LARRY PAGE
speech to Israeli students, 2003

I understand the appeal of a slow burn, but personally I'm a big-bang guy.

STEVE JOBS
Code Name Ginger, 2003

294

Nobody knows in business whether you're batting .320 or not so everybody says they're a .320 hitter. And the board of directors has to say, well, we've got a .320 hitter, because they couldn't be responsible for picking a guy that bats .250.

WARREN BUFFETT
remarks to the Financial Crisis Inquiry Commission, 2010

295

When I was 21, someone described Virgin as an "unprofessional professional organization," which for my money is just about the best backhanded compliment anyone in business could ever receive.

RICHARD BRANSON
Business Stripped Bare, 2008

296

Here's what I've learned: **If you don't ask for it, you're not likely to get it.**

OPRAH WINFREY
O, The Oprah Magazine, 2014

297

The world isn't going to tell you about great deals. You have to find them yourself.

WARREN BUFFETT
CNBC town hall meeting, 2009

298

Rationality
only goes
so far.

BILL GATES
Creative Capitalism, 2008

299

But periodically, every n years, you should work on something new that you think is really amazing. The trick is coming up with those products. I could probably give you a list of 10 major things that are wrong with email. I try to maintain lists like that in my head.

LARRY PAGE
Wired, 2013

300

[Computer coding is] iterative, right? You'll write it, then next year you'll write another story, and another, and eventually, the story will be the way you want it.

MARK ZUCKERBERG
Fast Company, 2012

The entrepreneurial mindset continues to thrive at Microsoft because one of our major goals is to reinvent ourselves—we have to make sure that we are the ones replacing our products instead of someone else.

BILL GATES
Industry Week, 1995

302

*The best, most
solid way out
of a crisis in a
changing market
is through
experiment and
adaptation.*

RICHARD BRANSON
Richard's blog, 2008

303

We come into work every
day knowing that we can
destroy the company . . .
and that we better keep our
wits about us, make the
long-term investments in
research that are going to
make a big difference and
really drive things forward.

———————

BILL GATES
keynote speech at San Jose State, 1998

304

Even if you fail at your ambitious thing, it's very hard to fail completely.

LARRY PAGE
In the Plex, 2011

305

Believe me, when somebody's in their entrepreneurial mode—being fanatical, inventing new things—the value they're adding to the world is phenomenal. If they invent new technologies, that is an amazing thing. And they don't even have to know how it's going to help people. But it will: in education, medical research, you name it.

BILL GATES
Technology Review, 2010

306

I don't think keeping the culture is a goal. I don't think we should be looking back to our golden years in the garage. The goal is to **improve as we grow**, and we certainly have more resources to bring to bear on the cultural issues and whatnot as we gain scale.

SERGEY BRIN
Fortune, 2008

307

Every three years are important in terms of redefining what we do. Any company that stays the same will be passed by very quickly and there are lots of fine examples of that.

BILL GATES
Smithsonian Institution Oral and Video Histories, 2003

308

As you grow your company, every time you increase by 50 percent it completely changes the culture and the way [you] have to organize.

LARRY PAGE
interview for FT Dynamo, 2001

309

Size works
against
excellence.
Even if we
are a big
company, we
cannot think
like a big
company or
we are dead.

BILL GATES
Financial Times, 1996

310

It's difficult for an elephant to step on all the ants because the ants won't allow it. They'll run here and there. And the elephant may break a leg trying to step on them all.

JACK MA
Beijing Morning Post, 2004

311

I do not believe in taking baby steps when you see something that you really understand. I never want to do anything on a small scale because, what's the reason? If I'm doing it on a small scale because I'm not that sure of my opinion, I'll forget it entirely and go on to something I'm sure about.

WARREN BUFFETT
colloquium at the University of Nebraska–Lincoln, 1994

312

THE BARRIER
TO CHANGE
IS NOT
TOO LITTLE
CARING; IT IS
**TOO MUCH
COMPLEXITY.**

BILL GATES
commencement address at Harvard University, 2007

It's important to simplify ... and take out everything that is secondary, to have less variables to study or to look at. Because when you have a lot of variables, and you don't make a distinction between the ones that are essential and the secondary ones ... you have confusion.

CARLOS SLIM
Academy of Achievement, 2007

We didn't need a lot of formal process because, believe me, it's better to have three guys who really know what's going on than to have all of the processes that allow twelve to all sort of think they are part of that decision process.

BILL GATES
Microsoft Rebooted, 2004

315

At a lot of big companies, **process becomes a substitute for thinking**. You're encouraged to behave like a little gear in a complex machine. Frankly, it allows you to keep people who aren't that smart, who aren't that creative.

ELON MUSK
Wired, 2012

316

We encourage our employees, in addition to their regular projects, to spend 20 percent of their time working on what they think will most benefit Google. This empowers them to be more creative and innovative. Many of our significant advances have happened in this manner.

LARRY PAGE AND SERGEY BRIN
Amendment 9 to Form S-1, 2004

317

What we do is not beyond anybody else's competence. I feel the same way about managing that I do about investing: It's just not necessary to do extraordinary things to get extraordinary results.

WARREN BUFFETT
Forbes, 1974

318

I think that there is more than one place where people can build companies. There's a feeling in Silicon Valley that you have to be there, because that's where all the engineers are. I just don't know if that's true. I think a lot of good companies get started all over the place.

MARK ZUCKERBERG
remarks at MIT, 2011

What I know
for sure is
that if you
want to have
success, you
can't make
success your
goal.

OPRAH WINFREY
O, The Oprah Magazine, 2001

320

We adhere always to placing the customer first, employees second, and shareholders third.

JACK MA
Alibaba's 10th anniversary celebration, 2009

If your business proposition is innovative, your ultimate goal has to be "The customer always thinks that we are right."

RICHARD BRANSON
Like a Virgin, 2012

322

I began life as a journalist, and I've always been sensitive to the fact that getting free coverage is one thing; deserving it is quite another.

RICHARD BRANSON
Reach for the Skies, 2010

323

Ultimately, you have to make money because you are a business. I let other people worry about that. I worry about the message. I am always, always, always about holding true to the vision and the message, and when you are true to that, then people respond.

OPRAH WINFREY
New York Times, 2012

324

We don't stand a chance of advertising with features and benefits and with RAMs and with charts and comparisons. The only chance we have of communicating is with a **feeling**.

STEVE JOBS
Return to the Little Kingdom, 2009

325

Whether in times of tragedy or joy, people want to share and help one another. This human need is what inspires us to continue to innovate and build things that allow people to connect easily and share their lives with one another.

MARK ZUCKERBERG
Facebook blog, 2010

The beauty of business is that it does not just have one single community.... The businesses that are most successful connect with everyone as an individual, not just as an order number or a transaction.

RICHARD BRANSON
Screw Business As Usual, 2011

The most important thing is a *person*—a person who incites your curiosity and feeds your curiosity; and machines cannot do that in the same way that people can.

STEVE JOBS
Smithsonian Institution Oral and Video Histories, 1995

328

The message that you get, in a lot of ways, is actually less important than who you get it from. If you get it from someone that you trust a lot more, then you really listen to it, whereas if you get it from someone you don't trust, you might actually believe the opposite of what they said because you don't trust them.

MARK ZUCKERBERG
Fast Company, 2009

329

Publicity is absolutely critical. You have to get your brand out and about, particularly if you're a consumer-oriented brand. . . . A good PR story is infinitely more effective than a full-page ad, and a damn sight cheaper.

RICHARD BRANSON
Business Stripped Bare, 2008

330

Advertising can help in recognition, but **branding is built by public response**. It's a cultural value that can never be hammered home by advertising alone.

JACK MA
Alibaba blog, 2012

I can't speak for other people, but dyslexia shaped my—and Virgin's—communication style. From the beginning, Virgin used clear, ordinary language. If I could quickly understand a campaign concept, it was good to go. **If something can't be explained off the back of an envelope, it's rubbish.**

RICHARD BRANSON
Forbes, 2012

332

Would I have been happy without my successes in business? I'd like to think so. But . . . it depends on what you mean by "business." Would I have been happy had I not found concerns to absorb me and fascinate me and engage me every minute of my life? No, absolutely not, I'd be as miserable as sin.

RICHARD BRANSON
Business Stripped Bare, 2008

333

A lot of times people think creating companies is going to be fun. I would say it's not. It's really not that fun. There are periods of fun, and there are periods where it's just awful. Particularly if you're the CEO of the company, you actually have a distillation of all the worst problems in the company. There's no point in spending your time on things that are going right, so you only spend your time on things that are going wrong.

ELON MUSK
Khan Academy Chats, 2013

334

I have created something that I enjoy....
It's a little crazy, it seems to me, if you
are building a business and creating a
business, not to create something you are
going to enjoy when you get through. It's
like painting a painting. I mean, you ought
to paint something you are going to enjoy
looking at when you get through.

WARREN BUFFETT
colloquium at the University of Nebraska–Lincoln, 1994

335

I really don't define my happiness by my business decisions.

OPRAH WINFREY
Fortune, 2002

336

REAL HAPPINESS . . . IS A PRODUCT OF WHO YOU ARE AND HOW YOU CONDUCT YOURSELF ON A DAILY BASIS.

CARLOS SLIM
commencement address at George Washington University, 2012

337

I am really good at working. Committed. Diligent. With stamina on steroids. Playing, I'm not so good at. I rarely decide to do anything just for fun. So the question I've recently started asking myself is, Am I having a good time? Am I doing what I really want? **What does fun look like?**

OPRAH WINFREY
O, The Oprah Magazine, 2015

338

From my parents, I certainly learned to be frugal and to be happy without very many things. It's interesting—I still find myself not wanting to leave anything on the plate uneaten. I still look at prices. I try to force myself to do this less, not to be so frugal. But I was raised being happy with not so much.

SERGEY BRIN
Moment, 2007

339

I think it would be very easy to get distracted and get caught up in short-term things or material things that don't matter. The phrase is actually, "Eliminating desire for all that doesn't really matter."

MARK ZUCKERBERG
Time, 2010

340

When we started, we'd be working upwards of 12 hours a day, 6 days a week. But we have been trying to cut down, because we think this isn't necessarily most productive. We try hard to take at least one of the weekend days off, and at times both or at least portions of both. Anyway, we're trying to push it down below 60 hours.

SERGEY BRIN
Stern magazine, 1999

I don't believe in working 20 hours or 16 hours or 14 hours. When you work too much, it is because your job is beyond you ... because you're not organized. You don't have delegation of your responsibility, and I don't believe that in any business, in any activity, you need to work 15 or 16 hours, and ... [not] have time for yourself or for your family or for anyone.

CARLOS SLIM
Academy of Achievement, 2007

342

I try not to waste time—because I don't want to waste myself. I'm working on not letting people with dark energy consume any of my minutes on this earth. I've learned that the hard way, after giving up hours of myself and my time, which are synonymous when you think about it.

OPRAH WINFREY
What I Know For Sure, 2014

343

Because there aren't enough hours in the day, it's tempting to try to do two things at once. Right now I'm perfecting reading a newspaper and riding an exercise bike at the same time—a very practical form of multitasking.

BILL GATES
New York Times, 1997

344

Donating money is important but not necessarily charitable. *Donating that of which you have the least is real charity.*

JACK MA
Jack Ma's Quotations on Entrepreneurship, 2008

When
you give,
do not
expect to
receive.

CARLOS SLIM
Carlosslim.com, 1994

346

There *is* such a thing as enlightened self-interest, and we should encourage it. It *is* possible to turn a profit while making the world a better place.

———

RICHARD BRANSON
Business Stripped Bare, 2008

I believe that the skills, the training, of the entrepreneur are very good to solve social and economic problems. Not because you have economic resources, or material resources, but because you know how to manage these resources. You understand how to solve problems.

CARLOS SLIM
Academy of Achievement, 2007

348

I am not a believer in just handing out
checks; you should run charity like
a business driving change. That is,
I believe that most people, even the
poorest and most deprived, don't just
want to be told what's good for them;
they want to be involved in helping to
make their own lives better.

RICHARD BRANSON
Screw Business As Usual, 2011

349

Capitalism is the only system that works, but it has its flaws; for one, it brings great wealth to only a few people. That wealth obviously brings extreme responsibility.

RICHARD BRANSON
O, The Oprah Magazine, 2007

350

For successful business leaders, if their goal is to be rich, they can become very rich. But then what's the point of having all that money? When you have 100 million U.S. dollars, I think that's more than enough for you and your children. Once your net worth exceeds a certain point, that's not your money anymore. It is society's money. It is the money society has given to you, and you should **take responsibility to allocate the money in a good way**.

JACK MA
Nature.org, 2009

351

A lot of people wait until later in their careers to think about how to give back, and I just had a bunch of conversations with my friends and people who I work with recently where it really occurred to me, "Why wait another 15 or 20 years when I'll have a lot more time to focus on it, but if we already have the resources we should probably get started on it now." Hopefully, participating in this encourages other people in our generation to do so as well.

MARK ZUCKERBERG
Time, 2010

352

I'm talking about the power of the **ordinary, everyday person** to become entrepreneurs and change-makers, to set up their own businesses, to seek their own fortune and be in control of their own lives, to say—screw business as usual, we can do it! We can turn things upside down and make a huge difference.

RICHARD BRANSON
Screw Business As Usual, 2011

353

The only reason
to be a person
whom everybody
knows, who
is successful,
is to transmit
the message of
successfulness,
to say, "That is
possible."

OPRAH WINFREY
Makers: Women Who Make America, 2013

354

Success is not to make money or to have companies or to be an outstanding professional. **The success is your life.** The success is your family, your friends. In this way I think I have been very successful, because of my sisters, my brothers, and especially because of my family, my children, my wife, and my friends. I think that's really success.

CARLOS SLIM
Academy of Achievement, 2007

355

Different companies care about different things. . . . For us, it is the mission: building a company that makes the world more open and connected. The articulation of that has, I think, changed over time. But that's really been, like, the belief the whole time.

MARK ZUCKERBERG
The Huffington Post, 2012

356

Just like me, your families brought you here, and you brought them here. Please keep them close and remember: They are what really matters in life.

LARRY PAGE
commencement address at the University of Michigan, 2009

357

Marry the right person. And I'm serious about that. It will make more difference in your life. It will change your aspiration, all kind of things. It's enormously important who you marry.

WARREN BUFFETT
CNBC town hall meeting, 2009

358

You will have a better
professional life with
a good personal life
and family life than if
you don't have a good
personal life and a
family life.

CARLOS SLIM
Academy of Achievement, 2007

359

At the end we depart with nothing; we leave behind only our work, family and friends, and, perhaps, a positive influence which we have planted.

CARLOS SLIM
Carlosslim.com, 1994

360

Business is not like a battlefield where you die and I win. In business, even if you die, I may not win.

JACK MA
World Economic Forum, 2015

361

If you don't
want to sell your
company, don't
get into a process
where you're
talking to people
about selling your
company.

MARK ZUCKERBERG
New York Times, 2012

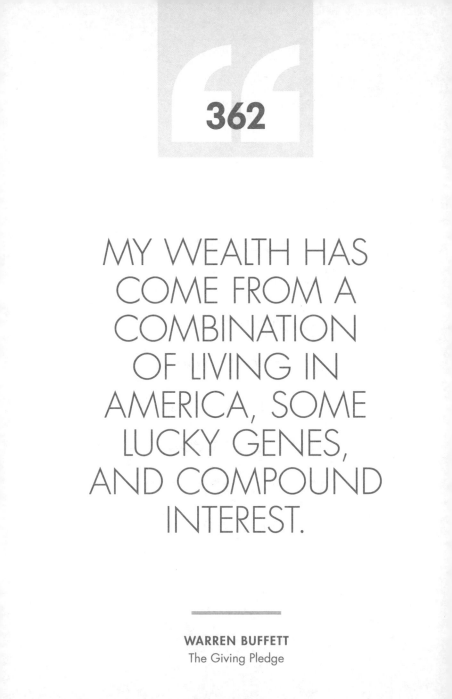

362

MY WEALTH HAS
COME FROM A
COMBINATION
OF LIVING IN
AMERICA, SOME
LUCKY GENES,
AND COMPOUND
INTEREST.

WARREN BUFFETT
The Giving Pledge

363

Being the richest man in the cemetery doesn't matter to me. . . . Going to bed at night saying we've done something wonderful . . . that's what matters to me.

STEVE JOBS
Wall Street Journal, 1993

364

I think what
matters is the
actions, not what
people think of
me in the future.
I'll be long dead.
But the actions
that I take, will
they have been
useful?

ELON MUSK
GQ, 2015

365

Let's go invent
tomorrow
rather than
worrying about
what happened
yesterday.

STEVE JOBS
D5 Conference, 2007

ACKNOWLEDGMENTS

I would like to thank my fellow editors who have contributed to the In Their Own Words series over the years: George Beahm, Lisa Rogak, David Andrews, Danielle McLimore, Tanni Haas, Suk Lee, Bob Song, Anjali Becker, and Jeanne Engelmann. These folks sifted through dozens upon dozens of documents and listened to hundreds of hours of appearances and interviews to find the best nuggets of wisdom for these books. I'd also like to give a shout-out to Helena Hunt, who helped me organize and prepare this volume. Thank you all!

For thousands of more inspiring and insightful quotes from today's most important entrepreneurs, collect all the books from Agate B2's In Their Own Words series, available at bookstores everywhere.

Praise for the In Their Own Words Series

I, STEVE: STEVE JOBS IN HIS OWN WORDS

"[It's] like eating salted peanuts:
Once you start reading, it's hard to stop."

—ANNE FISHER, *CNN MONEY*

OWN IT: OPRAH WINFREY IN HER OWN WORDS

"A choice pick for casual browsing, or as a source of inspiration for prospective entrepreneurs!"

—*MIDWEST BOOK REVIEW*

THE BOY BILLIONAIRE: MARK ZUCKERBERG IN HIS OWN WORDS

"*The Boy Billionaire* is nothing less than an authoritative portrait."

—*TECHNOMAG*